EVANSTON·PUBLIC
LIBRARY

Purchase of this library
material made possible
by a contribution
to the Fund for Excellence

21st Century Skills Library

GLOBAL PRODUCTS
DVDs

John Matthews

Cherry Lake Publishing
Ann Arbor, Michigan

Published in the United States of America by Cherry Lake Publishing
Ann Arbor, Michigan
www.cherrylakepublishing.com

Content Adviser: David Bunzel, President, Optical Storage Technology Association and
Managing Director, Santa Clara Consulting Group

Photo Credits: Cover and page 1, ©iStockphoto.com/jhorrocks; page 4, ©Tibor Bognar/
Alamy; page 7, ©Stavchansky Yakov, used under license from Shutterstock, Inc.; page
8, ©Mathieu Viennet, used under license from Shutterstock, Inc.; page 10, ©Aardvark/
Alamy; page 12, ©Richard Levine/Alamy; page 14 and 21, ©Simon Weir/Alamy; page 17,
©Kader Meguedad/Alamy; page 18, ©Enigma/Alamy; page 19, ©William Milner, used
under license from Shutterstock, Inc.; page 20, ©Simon Weir/Alamy; page 23, ©Oculo,
used under license from Shutterstock, Inc.; page 24, ©imagebroker/Alamy; page 26,
©Corbis Super RF/Alamy

Map by XNR Productions Inc.

Library of Congress Cataloging-in-Publication Data
Matthews, John, 1945–
  DVDs / by John Matthews.
    p. cm.
  Includes index.
  ISBN-13: 978-1-60279-253-1
  ISBN-10: 1-60279-253-4
  1. DVDs—Juvenile literature. 2. DVD players—Juvenile literature.
  3. Motion pictures—Juvenile literature. I. Title.
  TK7882.D93M38 2008
  621.388'332—dc22   2008014187

*Cherry Lake Publishing would like to acknowledge the work of
The Partnership for 21st Century Skills.
Please visit www.21stcenturyskills.org for more information.*

TABLE OF CONTENTS

CHAPTER ONE

FROM HOLLYWOOD TO BOLLYWOOD

*A billboard in Mysore, India, advertises a Bollywood movie.
DVDs make it much easier for cultures to share their media.*

Bryan walked to his grandparent's house. "Come on in Bryan," his
grandmother greeted him as he put his backpack on the hall table.
"Good news. Your mother says you can have dinner with us tonight. Go
back to the den. Your grandfather will want to know what you did in
school this week."

"Hi, Grandpa." Bryan looked at the DVDs sitting on the desk. "I see you have some new movies. Did you get anything for me to watch?"

"I always get movies with you in mind," Grandpa replied. "In fact, there's one you can take home and watch. It's a Bollywood film."

"What's Bollywood?"

"Bollywood is the 'Hollywood' of India," said Grandpa. "The film is called *Earth*, and it's about India and Pakistan becoming independent from United Kingdom. It's amazing the variety of films we can watch on DVDs. We'd never be able to see something like a Bollywood film down at the local movie theater. And people all over the world get to see our Hollywood films, too."

Then Grandpa added, "I suppose you need to spend some time on homework first. What assignments are you working on?"

"Our assignment is to research a product that is used all over the world and write as much about it as we can find. Then we get to talk about it in front of the class. I thought you might have some ideas about a product I can research."

"Why not research the product you're holding in your hand—DVDs?" Grandpa asked.

"What could I say about them after I point out that they're a plastic disc used to play movies?" Bryan responded.

"They're more than just a plastic disc," Grandpa said. "DVDs need a machine to record data and to play them. How was all that technology developed? Let's pretend you're making a movie about the DVD. I'll assign the questions to research, and you can do all the work."

"Okay, Grandpa, what's my first question?"

"What do the initials DVD stand for?"

Bryan sat down at Grandpa's computer and began his search. At dinner, he was ready with an answer. "DVD used to stand for Digital Video Disc. However, because DVDs can be used for other purposes, it really means Digital Versatile Disc. One source I found says it doesn't stand for anything. DVD just means DVD."

"I'll bet you found out a lot of other information about DVDs, didn't you?" Grandpa asked. "The other students are going to want to know how DVDs work."

"Grandpa, do you think we could open

up the cover of your DVD player to see how it works?"

"I think there's a better way," Grandpa said. "Why don't you first research more to find out who invented the DVD and how DVDs play recorded movies. Then I'll give you the next assignment."

Netflix was founded in 1997 by Reed Hastings and has grown into a successful multimillion dollar business. It has changed the way people rent DVD movies. Netflix pioneered a unique system of online and mail-order DVD rental. In 1999, it established a rental policy of no late fees, no shipping or handling fees, and no per-title rental fee.

Hastings is an example of how an individual with a good idea can establish a highly successful business. Can you think of ideas no one else has thought of that might be turned into successful businesses?

DVD players come in different sizes. Those that are portable have rechargeable batteries and don't need to be plugged in while in use.

CHAPTER TWO

WHO INVENTED DVD?

*The invention of videocassette tapes paved the way
for a whole new industry: video rental stores.*

The following week, Bryan was ready with the first part of his research report. "I discovered that DVDs were developed to replace videotape cassettes. Videotape cassettes were invented so people could rent movies to watch on television. And I learned something about how things are invented, too."

"Good." Grandpa looked pleased. "Tell me about it."

Bryan explained that it's not always clear who is responsible for creating a new product. Sometimes inventors use other inventors' work to develop a product. The movie camera, for instance, could not have been invented if someone had not already invented film in long strips that could be wound around a spool. Movies would have remained silent without the invention of technology that allowed music and conversation to be recorded and played back.

○ ○ ○

DVD is only one of several kinds of **optical discs**. David Paul Gregg invented the first optical disc in the late 1950s. His disc worked by recording data or images in the form of pits or bumps on the surface of the disc in one continuous spiral. To play back the disc, a **laser** light in the player shines onto the pits and bumps and turns them into the images we see.

Gregg first **patented** his disc in 1961. MCA DiscoVision bought his patents along with his company. In 1978, MCA marketed the first optical disc. It was popularly known as a Laserdisc. This Laserdisc was used mostly for recording movies for viewing in people's homes.

Sony's main headquarters are in Japan, but the company has offices around the world, including the United Kingdom headquarters near Weybridge, England.

After Gregg invented the Laserdisc, various electronics companies began separately developing the technology for the optical disc. In 1995, three companies—Philips, Sony, and Toshiba—agreed on a standard format for the optical disc, the DVD. This is the standard used for all DVDs today.

The first DVD players went on sale in Japan in 1996. Philips, a Dutch company, introduced its player to the U.S. market in 1997. Philips makes players in China and sells them throughout the world.

21st Century Content

Ten major international companies that market DVD players and recorders formed a group called the DVD Forum. The creation of this group was inspired by an agreement on a standard format for DVDs by Philips, Sony, and Toshiba. The forum's members agreed to industry manufacturing standards for the DVD.

The forum is responsible for official DVD format specifications. It handles the many licenses of DVD technology so that players and discs are **compatible** with each other. There are many forum members today and some minor differences in their products. By working together as an industry, they created standards that allowed for DVD discs to be used in most players around the world.

Do you think all international companies should agree to the same standards for the products they produce? Why or why not?

CHAPTER THREE

THE DISC COMES FIRST

Large electronics stores stock hundreds of popular items, such as affordable DVD players.

"**I** think it's time for a field trip," Grandpa told Bryan the following week.

"I like field trips," Bryan said, remembering his trip to the science museum with his fifth-grade class. "Where are we going?"

"We're going to an electronics store."

"Sounds like we're going shopping!" Bryan exclaimed.

"Oh, we're not going to buy anything," Grandpa said. "But if you're going to learn everything there is to know about DVD technology, it will help to see all the DVD products displayed in one place."

"Sounds like the perfect way to compare and contrast," Bryan said. "That's exactly what I'm supposed to do in my report. Let's go!"

At the store, the DVD players were lined up according to price. The lowest price was $29.98 for a small player. The highest price was $240 for a larger player/recorder combination.

"It's amazing," Grandpa said. "I remember when DVD players first came out. They cost $600 or more, and now you can get one for $30. DVDs are a great example of products that go through a life cycle. Early in the cycle they may cost a lot, but they get more affordable over time."

○ ○ ○

Philips Electronics, a global company, is the primary inventor of recordable discs, commonly referred to as DVDs. Philips markets its own brand of recordable discs. Disc manufacturers in Taiwan—such as CMC Magnetics, Ritek, and Prodisc Technology—pay a license fee to Philips for use of its patent. Most recordable discs are made in China, Taiwan, and India. Some recordable discs are single-sided, and some are double-sided. The recordable disc consists of several layers.

Dual layers of a DVD are bonded together on an automated production line.

The single-sided disc has the recordable layer on one side and the label on the other.

The recordable disc is made up of several layers. These include a reflective layer. This layer often uses a precious metal such as gold or silver along with a special dye that changes when the laser is focused on it.

A DVD player, such as those sold by Philips, has three major components: a motor to spin the disc, a laser and lens to focus and read the bumps of data, and a tracking mechanism to guide the laser along the tracks and across the disc. The laser beam shines onto the reflective layer of the disc that contains the bumps. The bumps reflect back the light that is converted into an image. The tracking mechanism keeps the laser centered on the track. As the tracks spiral outward from the center toward the edge of the disc, the data bumps move past the laser at an increasing speed. The motor must then slow the spinning of the disc so that the bumps pass the laser beam at a constant speed.

21st Century Content

Royal Philips Electronics (commonly known as Philips) is the company that introduced DVD players in the United States. Philips owns many of the technologies used in the design and manufacture of the discs, players, and recorders. It is a global company with headquarters in Amsterdam, Netherlands. It has major divisions in the United States, the United Kingdom, Mexico, and India. Philips products are sold all over the world.

What are the advantages of a company having offices all over the world? Do you think there are also disadvantages?

CHAPTER FOUR

Using DVDs

Advances in manufacturing technology and DVD technology helped make it possible to produce millions of DVDs of a single movie.

"You've learned a lot by researching DVDs," Grandpa said. "Have you learned all the ways DVDs are used?"

"Well, I know they're mostly used by movie studios to make movies for sale or rent," Bryan said. "What I don't know is how the movies are put on the discs."

A video editor digitally manipulates film clips. Arranging clips of film footage requires a good eye for detail.

"No problem!" said Grandpa. "I just happen to have a friend who is a video editor who prepares videos for DVDs. Want to meet her?"

"For sure! Let's go!"

A reflective coating is applied to a DVD during manufacturing.

English. Menus can also be prepared for different scenes within the movie so the viewer can easily locate these scenes.

The editor sends these files, known as **pre-master** files, to the DVD manufacturer. The finished pre-master files are sent to a company that makes a **glass master**. The glass master is spin coated with a light-sensitive substance called photoresist. It is then baked until hardened and ready for exposure to a laser beam. The laser recorder transfers data from the pre-master files to the glass master. This creates pits on the surface. The pits become the DVD's playable image when the DVD player's laser beam shines on them.

In the next stage of the disc manufacturing process, a stamper presses the playable image onto thousands of blank plastic discs. A thin metal reflective layer is put onto the surface of each disc and coated with protective lacquer. The layers are then pressed together and placed under **infrared** light. The DVD is now finished and ready to play.

This is called the pressed, or replication, method of manufacture. It does not use premade recordable discs such as those found in electronics stores. It makes the disc from scratch. This method is suitable for making large quantities—many thousands—of discs and is used for manufacturing movie DVDs.

People who study **marketing** talk about the life cycle of a product. Some products have a short life cycle. One example of a product with a short life cycle is the **pager**. It has largely been replaced by the cell phone.

Other products have long life cycles. One product with a long life cycle is the automobile. It has been continuously improved since its invention in the late 19th century and remains as popular as ever.

Do you think the DVD will have a long life cycle or a short life cycle? Why?

21st Century Content

As the movie industry switched their home video sales and rentals from videotape cassettes to DVD discs, stores that sold and rented videocassettes had to quickly switch as well. Some stores were successful at doing this, while others were not and went out of business.

Blockbuster is one company that successfully made the change from videocassettes to DVDs. Blockbuster stores opened in 1985. In 2007, Blockbuster had more than 5,000 stores in the United States and more than 2,600 stores in foreign countries.

What do you think stores like Blockbuster must do to remain successful when they have to quickly change the kinds of products they offer?

Another manufacturing method is called recorded disc manufacture, or duplication. It begins with recordable blank DVD discs. Data from a disc or a computer file is written, or burned, onto blank discs using a DVD writer, a high-speed device that records multiple discs. On the computer, this device is called a **DVD-ROM drive**. This method is preferred for manufacturing quantities fewer than 1,000 discs.

CHAPTER FIVE

THE FUTURE IS ALREADY HERE

Phonograph records are played on a record player, or a turntable.

"Just think, Grandpa, DVDs have replaced videocassettes, just like music CDs replaced phonograph records."

"Whoa, Bryan! DVDs haven't entirely replaced videocassettes," said

A Blu-ray disc can store about 5 times more data than a regular DVD.

Grandpa. "Many of the players still in use today are combinations of DVD and cassette players."

"What do you think will replace DVDs in the future?" Bryan asked.

"I think the future of the DVD is already here," said Grandpa. "It may not be replaced entirely, but it will be transformed by better technology.

In other words, today's DVDs are already changing because of changes in other products. Remember our discussion of product life cycles? A new life cycle of recorded video may have already started. I'm talking about Blu-ray Disc."

"Tell me more, Grandpa," said Bryan. "I can finish my report on a product used all over the world by talking about the beginning of a new global product!"

○ ○ ○

Blu-ray Discs represent the next generation of DVD. They complement the new high-definition television format (HDTV). The basic technology is similar to the optical disc now used for DVD.

Blu-ray uses a blue laser with a shorter wavelength than a regular DVD. It can store about 25 **gigabytes** on a single-sided disc, as opposed to the 4.7 gigabytes that can be stored on a regular DVD. The first retail Blu-ray players were introduced in stores in the United States in 2002. The introductory price was about $1,000. Because **copy protection** for the format had not been developed, no movies were issued at that time for Blu-ray players. The device was too expensive for the average consumer, so the manufacturer marketed a version of Blu-ray to businesses for data storage. Now Blu-ray players can be found in retail stores. Movie discs made for the players are also becoming more available and popular.

Downloaded movies don't require a disc. They can be watched directly from the computer they were transferred to.

Another development is the growing availability of movies that can be **downloaded** from the Internet. For prices similar to DVD rental or purchase, customers can download movie files to their computer hard drives. Movies can then be viewed directly from the downloaded files or transferred to a recordable disc. Movies rented this way have codes embedded in the file. These codes will prevent the movie from being viewed after a certain time or after a certain number of viewings. Movies that are purchased instead of rented often can be burned to a disc without limitations on time or viewings.

○ ○ ○

"I think it's time we enjoyed watching a movie together," Grandpa said.

Bryan looked at all the DVDs there were to choose from.

"Just think, Grandpa," said Bryan. "We could be watching a DVD movie that was filmed in Mexico with the words in English. Maybe it was transferred to a DVD in the United States, manufactured in China, and brought to the United States on a ship from Singapore. And that same ship will take copies of the same movie to other countries. Thanks for helping me discover that DVDs are a product people all over the world use and enjoy!"

21st Century Content

According to In-Stat and the Santa Clara Consulting Group—two companies that track technology trends—the standard DVD market may be nearing its peak. It is facing competition not only from the new high-definition optical discs, but also from Internet downloads and from pay-TV companies that want to add movies to their growing HDTV services.

Can you think of other ways that DVDs might be used in the future besides for movies and music entertainment?

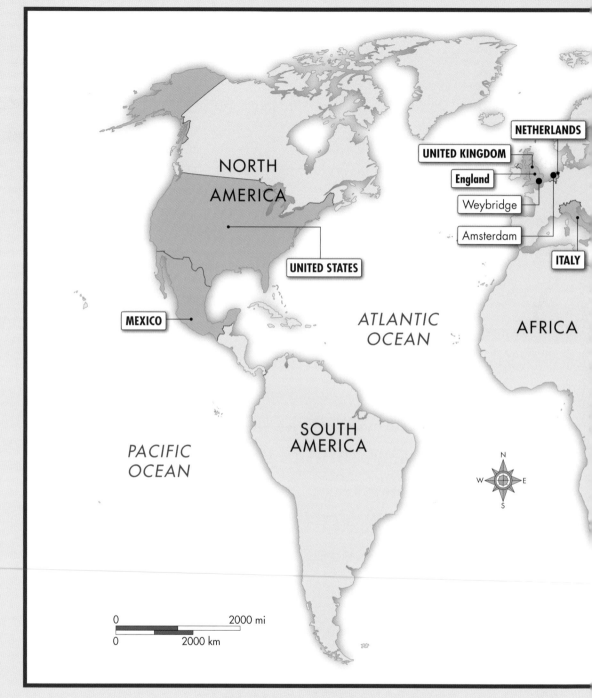

NORTH AMERICA

UNITED KINGDOM

NETHERLANDS

England

Weybridge

Amsterdam

ITALY

UNITED STATES

MEXICO

ATLANTIC OCEAN

AFRICA

PACIFIC OCEAN

SOUTH AMERICA

N
W · E
S

0   2000 mi
0   2000 km

This map shows the countries and cities mentioned in the text.

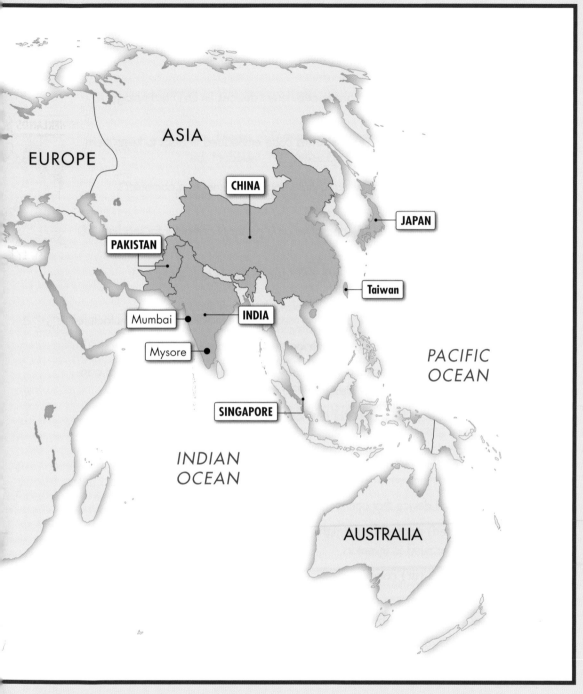

They are the locations of some of the companies involved in the making and selling of DVDs.

INDEX

ABOUT THE AUTHOR

John Matthews began a new career as an author after a career as a book publisher. He has written numerous books about inventions, wildlife, and history. John loved going to movie theaters when he was growing up. Today, he is an avid DVD movie fan who loves getting to watch movies at home. "I enjoyed writing this book because I discovered so many things about one of my favorite things."